D0643493

Make Origami
AMPHIBIANS

by Ruth Owen

PowerKiDS press
New York

Published in 2018 by **The Rosen Publishing Group, Inc.**
29 East 21st Street, New York, NY 10010

CATALOGING-IN-PUBLICATION DATA
Names: Owen, Ruth.
Title: Make origami amphibians / Ruth Owen.
Description: New York : PowerKids Press, 2018. | Series: Animal kingdom origami |
     Includes index.
Identifiers: ISBN 9781499433517 (pbk.) | ISBN 9781499433456 (library bound) |
     ISBN 9781499433333 (6 pack)
Subjects: LCSH: Origami--Juvenile literature. | Amphibians in art--Juvenile literature.
Classification: LCC TT872.5 O94 2018 | DDC 736'.982--dc23

First Edition

Produced for Rosen by Ruth Owen Books

Designer: Emma Randall
Photo Credits: Courtesy of Ruth Owen Books and Shutterstock.

Manufactured in the United States of America
CPSIA Compliance Information: Batch BS17PK: For Further Information contact Rosen Publishing, New York, New York at 1-800-237-9932.

Contents

What Is an Amphibian?

There are more than 7,000 different **species** of amphibians. This animal group includes frogs, toads, caecilians, salamanders, and newts, which are a type of salamander. Most amphibians spend part of their lives in water and part on land.

Tree frog

Amphibians are **ectothermic**, or cold-blooded. This means the animal's body cannot **regulate** its inner temperature. As the air or water around an amphibian gets warmer or colder, the animal's inner body temperature goes up or down, too.

Salamander

Caecilian

A frog's skeleton

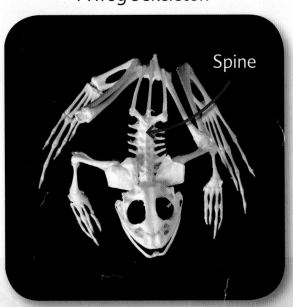

Spine

Amphibians are **vertebrates**, which means they have a backbone, or spine.

Amphibians begin their lives as eggs. Then they go through changes, known as a **metamorphosis**.

A newt larva underwater

Gills

After the egg stage of its life, an amphibian becomes a **larva**. It lives in water and breathes through body parts called **gills**. The gills take in **oxygen** from the water.

An adult newt

In time, the larva changes and becomes an adult. Once they are adults, most amphibians live on land. They have lungs and breathe air.

Get ready to fold and learn more about amphibians!

5

Frogs: Amphibians That Jump

There are almost 4,800 different species of frogs on Earth. Using their back legs, most frogs are able to make long jumps, or leaps. Frogs can also walk, climb, and swim in order to move from place to place.

Yellow-banded poison dart frog

Step 1:

Fold the paper in half diagonally, crease, and unfold. Then fold the paper diagonally in the opposite direction, crease, and unfold.

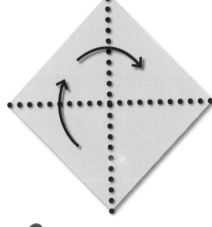

FOLD A JUMPING FROG

You will need:
- *A square piece of paper in your choice of color or pattern*
- *Markers*

Step 2:

Now fold the four points into the center.

Step 3:

Next, fold the two side points of the model into the center to form a kite shape.

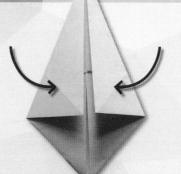

Then fold up the bottom point.

Step 4:

Now fold the two sides of the model into the center, and crease hard.

Step 5:

Fold up the bottom of the model, and crease hard.

Step 6:

Fold the bottom of the model back down along the dotted line, and crease hard. Fold down the top point of the model.

Flick downward here

Step 7:

Turn the model over and your jumping frog is ready.

Use markers to decorate the frog model.

To make the frog jump, flick the back of the model. Your frog will probably turn a somersault, too!

Tadpoles: A Frog's Life Cycle

A frog's life cycle has three stages: egg, larva, and adult. A frog larva is known as a tadpole. A female frog lays her eggs in water. Each tiny black egg is surrounded by jelly. The eggs become tadpoles that wriggle out of the jelly. The tiny tadpoles have tails and look more like fish than frogs.

A tadpole forming

Jelly

Tadpole

FOLD A TADPOLE

You will need:
• A small square piece of paper in your choice of color
• A black marker

Step 1:

Fold the paper in half diagonally, and crease.

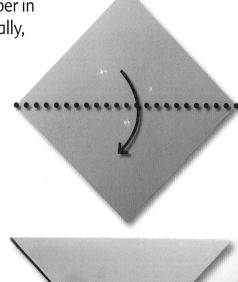

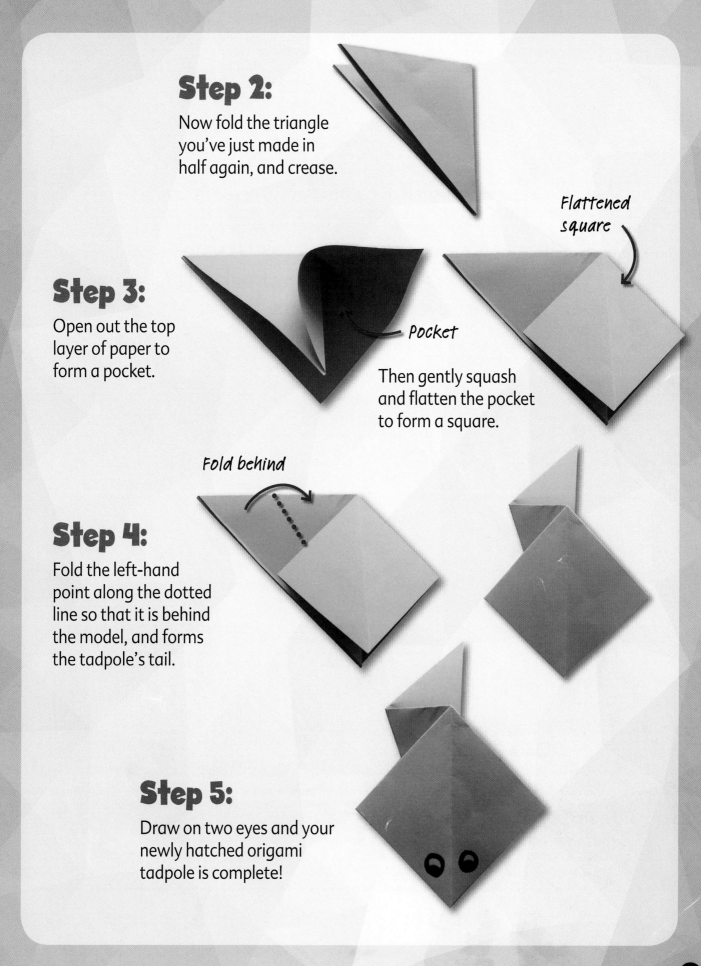

Step 2:

Now fold the triangle you've just made in half again, and crease.

Flattened square

Step 3:

Open out the top layer of paper to form a pocket.

Pocket

Then gently squash and flatten the pocket to form a square.

Fold behind

Step 4:

Fold the left-hand point along the dotted line so that it is behind the model, and forms the tadpole's tail.

Step 5:

Draw on two eyes and your newly hatched origami tadpole is complete!

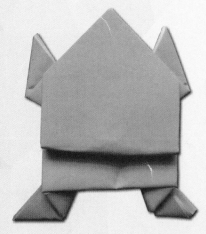

A tadpole goes through a lot of changes to become a frog. First, it grows back legs. Then its front legs grow. Its tail gets shorter and shorter and its body and head become more froglike.

As a tadpole becomes a frog, its lungs develop so it can breathe air and no longer breathe through its gills. Once its metamorphosis is complete, a tadpole leaves the water as a tiny froglet. Then it grows bigger and bigger and becomes an adult frog.

Tadpole with back legs

Tadpole with front and back legs

Froglet

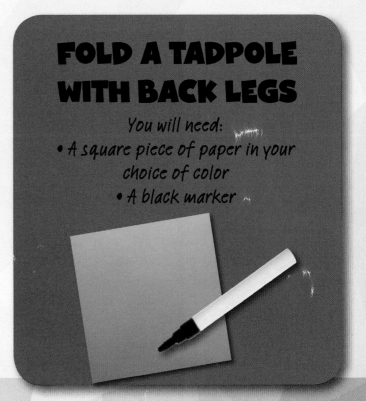

(Learn how to make this model on pages 14 to 17.)

FOLD A TADPOLE WITH BACK LEGS

You will need:
- A square piece of paper in your choice of color
- A black marker

Step 1:

Fold the paper in half diagonally, and crease. Then fold in half again.

Step 2:

Open out the top layer of paper to create a pocket.

Then gently squash and flatten the pocket to form a square.

Pocket

Square

Turn the model over. Open up the right-hand point of the model, and then squash it flat to form a square.

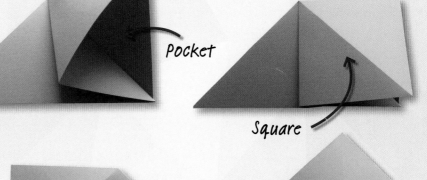

Open up the pocket here

Open edge

Open edge

Step 3:

Working with just the top layer of paper, fold in the two side points, and crease hard.

Then fold down the top point, and crease hard.

Now open out the three folds you've just made to create a beak-like shape.

Beak-like shape

Then gently squash and fold down the paper to form a diamond.

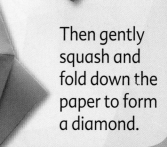

11

Step 4:

Turn the model over. Then repeat what you did in step 3 by folding in the three points, and creasing hard.

Then open out the three folds you've just made and squash them flat to create a diamond shape.

Step 5:

Now fold down the top point of the paper.

Your model should now look like this.

Step 6:

Turn the model over and you will have two legs at the bottom.

Slightly open out the right-hand side of the model and reverse fold the right-hand leg.

Right-hand leg

A reverse fold

Left-hand leg

Then repeat on the left-hand leg.

Fold down the tips of the legs.

Step 7:

Fold down the top point of the model.

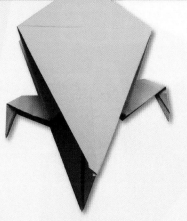

Step 8:

Turn the model 90 degrees counterclockwise. Then fold it in half.

Your model should look like this.

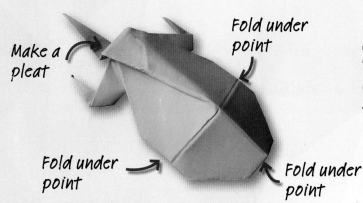

(We've used a paperclip just to hold this thick fold in place for our photo.)

Step 9:

Now fold up the bottom of the model, as shown. You are working with several layers of paper and will need to crease hard!

Step 10:

Next slightly open out the body of the tadpole. The fold you made in step 9 will have given the body a three-dimensional effect.

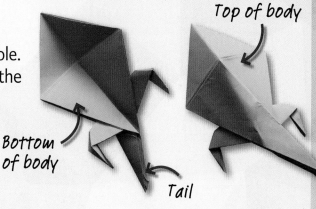

Top of body

Bottom of body

Tail

Step 11:

Make a small pleat in the tail.

Make a pleat

Fold under point

Fold under point

Fold under point

Then to round off the body, fold under the three points as shown.

Step 12:

Complete your origami tadpole by drawing on eyes.

Toads: Lumpy, Bumpy Amphibians

Toads are amphibians with dry skin that's covered in wart-like bumps. Toads generally walk from place to place, rather than hopping like their frog relatives.

Female toads lay their eggs in ponds. The eggs become tadpoles which live in water. As adults, toads live on land in forests, grasslands, and even in backyards.

Toads shelter in **burrows** in cool places such as under large stones or logs. In winter, a toad may go into its burrow, dig down into the soil, and then stay underground until spring. Toads feed on many different foods, including insects, spiders, earthworms, and slugs.

FOLD A TOAD

You will need:
- A square piece of green paper
- Colored markers

STEP 1:

Fold the paper in half, and crease.

STEP 2:

Fold over the top left-hand corner of the model, crease, and then unfold. Repeat on the top right-hand corner.

STEP 3:

Now fold over the top of the model. You should fold at the place where the creases you made in step 2 meet. Then unfold.

STEP 4:

Take hold of the two sides of the model at the top and begin to squash them into the center. As you do this, the creases you've made will make the top of the model collapse into a triangle.

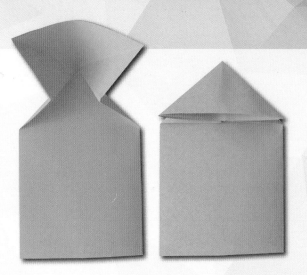

STEP 5:

To make the toad's front legs, fold up the two bottom points of the triangle along the dotted lines, and crease hard.

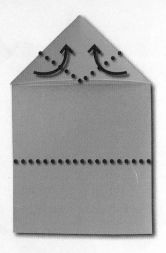

Then fold up the bottom half of the model, and crease.

STEP 6:

Now fold in the sides of the model so that they meet in the center. Crease hard.

STEP 7:

Fold up the bottom of the model, and crease hard. Now open out the bottom of the model to make a pocket. Squash down and flatten the pocket against the model.

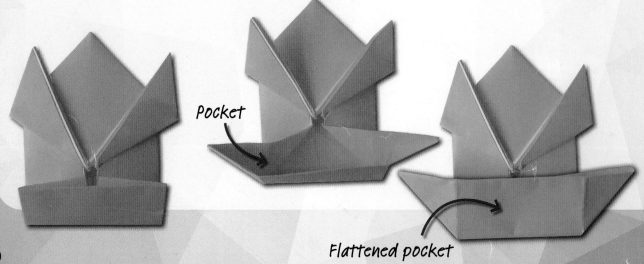

Pocket

Flattened pocket

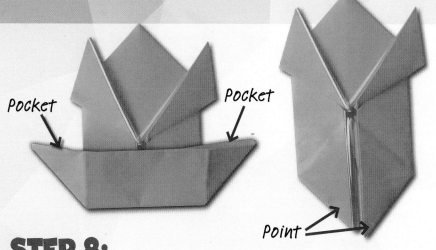

Pocket

Pocket

Point

STEP 8:

Next, open out one of the side pockets at the bottom of the model. Then squash and flatten it down to create a point. Repeat on the other side.

Then fold back each point to create the toad's back legs.

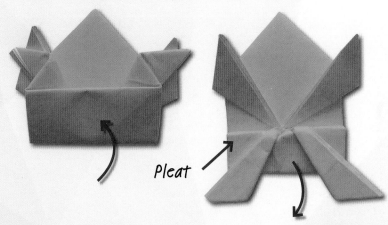

Pleat

STEP 9:

Fold up the bottom of the model, and crease hard. Then fold it back down again, making a small pleat.

STEP 10:

Flip the model over and your toad is complete. If you wish, draw colorful warty lumps on your toad.

You can also make a frog using these instructions.

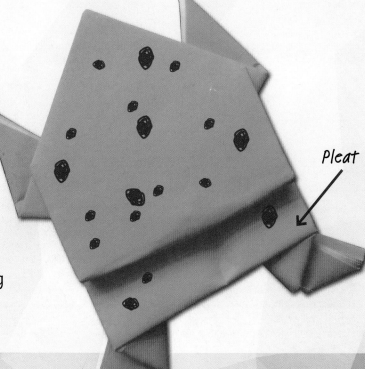

Pleat

Salamanders: Amphibians with Tails

Salamanders are amphibians with lizard-like bodies. They have a long tail and four short legs. Some species of salamanders are less than an inch (3 cm) long. The Chinese giant salamander can grow to more than 5 feet (2 m) long. It is the largest amphibian on Earth.

As adults, some species of salamanders live on land, while others spend time in water and on land. Some types of salamanders, including the Chinese giant salamander, are actually **aquatic**. These animals live in water both as a larva and as an adult.

A fire salamander

18

FOLD A SALAMANDER

You will need:
- 2 square pieces of paper in your choice of color or pattern
- Scissors

Step 1:

Fold a square of paper in half diagonally, crease, and unfold. Then fold the paper diagonally in the opposite direction, crease, and unfold.

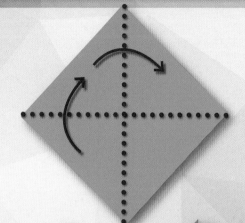

Step 2:

Fold the bottom and top of the paper into the center crease to make a kite shape. Crease and then unfold.

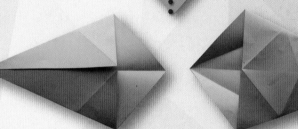

Next, fold in the top and bottom from the other direction, as shown, and crease.

Step 3:

Turn the model over. Fold up the bottom point to meet the top point, and crease.

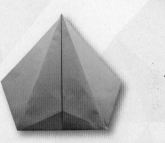

Step 4:

Turn the model over again.

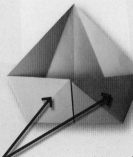

Pockets

Now fold down the pocket on the right-hand side to form a point.

Repeat on the left-hand side, and you will have created another kite shape.

19

Step 5:

Turn the model 90 degrees counterclockwise. Then fold the top left-hand point over to the right.

Your model should now look like this.

Step 6:

Fold the top and bottom points into the center of the model, and crease.

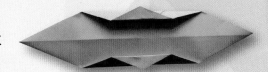

Step 7:

Then fold the top and bottom points back out again to the edges of the model.

Step 8:

Turn the model over and fold out the two center points to create the salamander's front legs.

Step 9:

Fold in the left-hand point of the model to meet the legs.

Step 10:

Unfold the left-hand point and open it out. Next, carefully fold back and flatten the edges of the paper.

As you do this, fold over and flatten the end point.

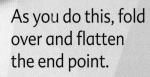

Your model should look like this.

Step 11:

Fold over the end of the model along the dotted line, and crease hard.

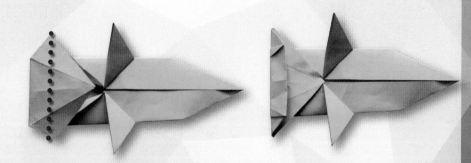

Step 12:

Now fold the top of the model into the center along the dotted lines, crease hard, and unfold. Then repeat on the bottom.

Step 13:

Next, fold in the edges of the right-hand point to form the salamander's tail.

Turn the model over, and the salamander's body is complete.

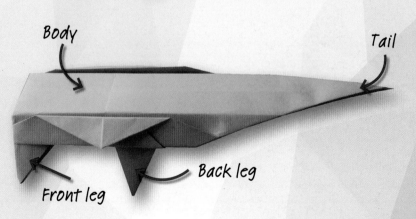

Body

Tail

Front leg

Back leg

Step 14:

To make the salamander's head take a square of paper that's a quarter the size of the square you used to make the body. Fold the paper in half, crease, and unfold.

Turn the paper over and fold the bottom and top into the center crease.

Step 16:

Turn the paper over again and you'll have an accordion effect. Close up the bottom half of the accordion.

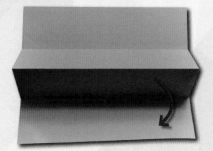

Step 17:

Fold in the four corners, and crease hard.

Step 18:

Fold up the bottom half of the model, and crease hard.

You will have created a small pocket.

Step 19:

Now fold the model in half to create a center crease, and unfold. Make a small cut in the crease you've just made.

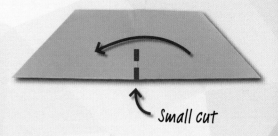

Small cut

Step 20:

Using the small cut you've just made, fold back the four edges of the pocket.

Inside of pocket

Then close up the pocket to create the salamander's head. Use a little glue to hold the jaws closed.

Step 21:

Finally glue the head to the body, and fold out the four legs.

Your origami salamander is complete!

Axolotls: Odd-Looking Amphibians

The axolotl is a type of salamander. It's name is pronounced ax-oh-lot-ul. These animals come in many different colors, including black, pink, and white.

An axolotl never goes through a metamorphosis. It hatches from its egg as a tiny, **transparent** larva with a tail and no legs. The larva then grows legs and gets bigger and bigger until it is about 10 inches (25 cm) long. Unlike frogs, toads, and other types of salamanders, however, an axolotl's body doesn't change form as it becomes an adult. This amphibian **breeds** and lives its whole life in its larval form. It breathes through gills and is aquatic, spending all its time in water.

FOLD AN AXOLOTL

You will need:
- Several square pieces of paper in your choice of colors
- Scissors • Markers

Step 1:

This model is made from 26 separate pieces, or modules.

A module

Step 2:

To make the axolotl's body we used four modules. Each module was made from a piece of rectangular paper measuring 4 inches by 5 inches (10 x 13 cm).

Step 3:

To make a module, fold the rectangular paper in half.

Then fold it in half again.

Step 4:

Now fold up the right-hand side of the model into the center, and crease.

Repeat on the left-hand side.

STEP 5:

Turn the model over. Fold down the two outer top corners, and crease.

STEP 6:

Next, fold down the top two flaps, creasing hard.

STEP 7:

Now close up the module. It should have two points and two slots.

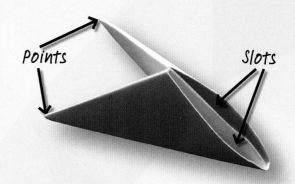

Points

Slots

STEP 8:

Make three more modules for the body.

To make the axolotl's legs, you will need 20 small modules. We used rectangles of paper that measured 2 inches by 3 inches (5 x 8 cm).

STEP 9:

To make the axolotl's gills, take a piece of paper that's 2 inches by 4 inches (5 x 10 cm).

Fold the paper on the long edge six times, making narrow folds to create an accordion effect. Then cut the folded paper in half.

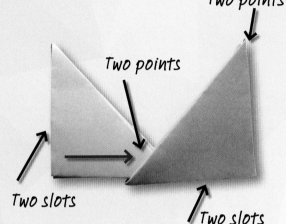

Two points

Two points

Two slots

Two slots

STEP 10:

Now begin assembling your model. We took a purple body module and a pink body module.

Tuck the two points of the purple module inside the pink module. Then slide the two modules together. You should now have slots at the bottom and on the left-hand side.

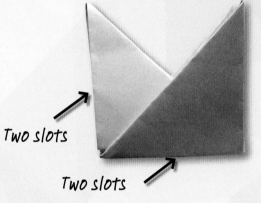

Two slots

Two slots

STEP 11:

Turn the model 90 degrees clockwise. Take a second purple module and slide it onto the two points of the pink module.

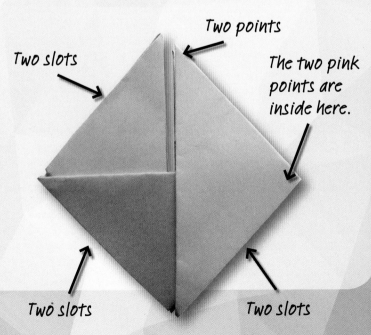

Two slots

Two points

The two pink points are inside here.

Two slots

Two slots

27

STEP 12:

Slide on the final pink module.

Tuck the two pink points into the purple module.

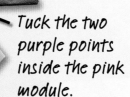
Two slots

Tuck the two purple points inside the pink module.

Then gently press and slide the four modules together until they are tightly joined.

STEP 13:

Now take a small leg module. Slide the two points into the two slots on one side of the body. Push in firmly.

STEP 14:

Add four more leg modules. Each time, slide the points into the slots of the previous module.

You can slightly curve the leg.

STEP 15:

Add a leg to each of the body modules.

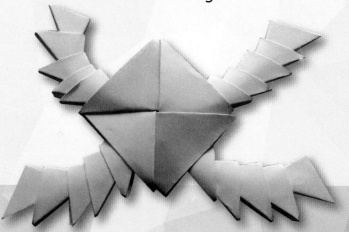

STEP 16:

Choose a corner of the model to be the axolotl's head. Then tuck the two gills into the body modules.

To complete your model, draw on eyes and a mouth.

Glossary

aquatic
Living in water.

breeds
Mates with a partner and produces young.

burrows
Underground animal homes.

ectothermic
Cold-blooded and not able to maintain a constant inner body temperature.

gills
The organs of amphibians and fish that extract oxygen from water.

larva
A young animal that has hatched from an egg. The young of amphibians, fish, and insects are known as larvae.

metamorphosis
The process of transforming from one thing to another. A tadpole goes through a metamorphosis to become a frog or toad.

oxygen
An invisible gas in air and in water that most living things need for survival.

regulate
To adjust the temperature up or down to keep it at the same level.

species
One type of living thing. The members of a species look alike and can produce young together.

transparent
See-through.

vertebrates
Animals with spines, or backbones, and a skeleton of other bones.

Websites

Due to the changing nature of internet links, PowerKids Press has developed an online list of websites related to the subject of this book. This site is updated regularly. Please use this link to access the list:

www.powerkidslinks.com/ako/amphibians

Index